PEGASUS ENCYCLOPEDIA LIBRARY

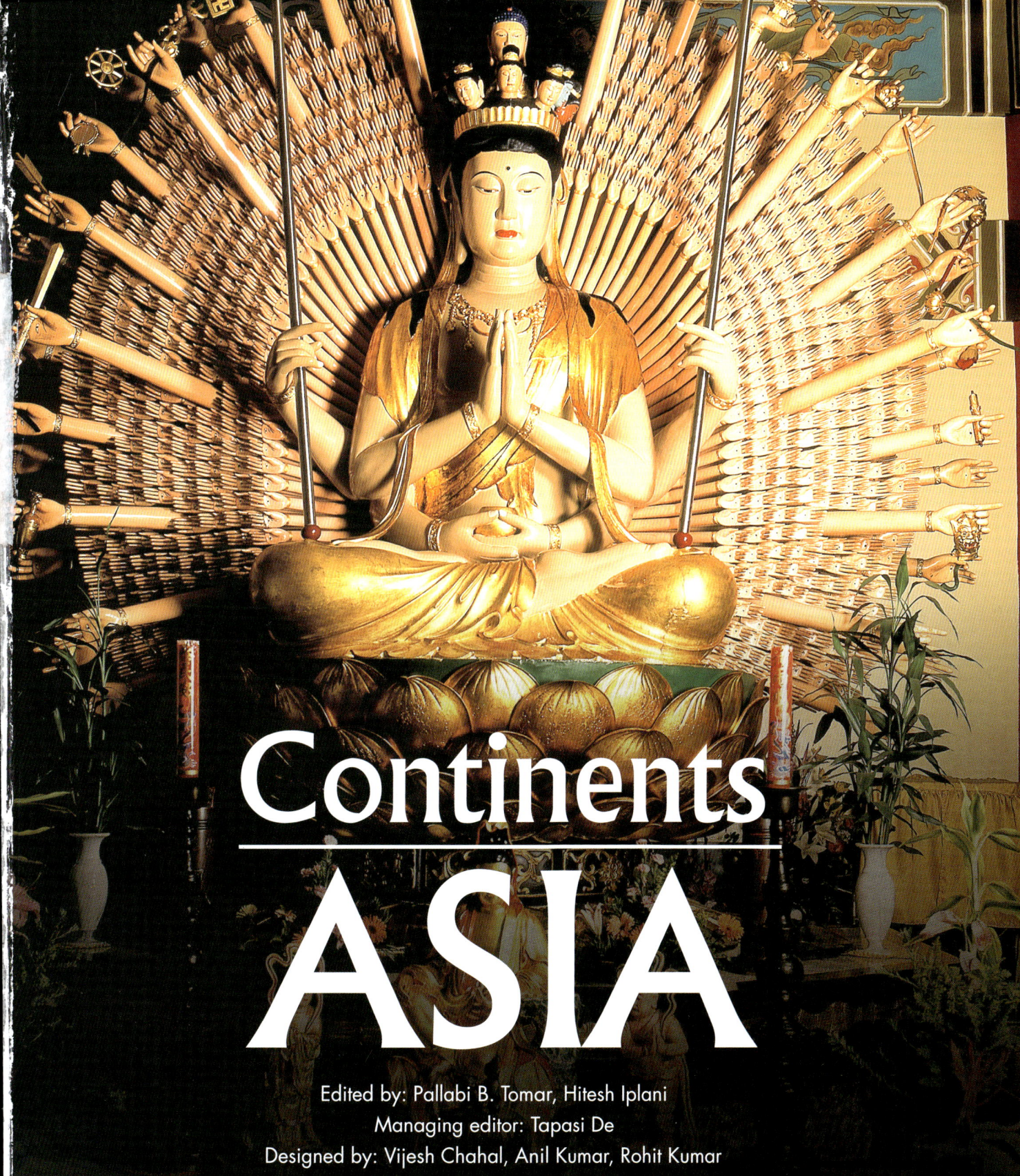

Continents
ASIA

Edited by: Pallabi B. Tomar, Hitesh Iplani
Managing editor: Tapasi De
Designed by: Vijesh Chahal, Anil Kumar, Rohit Kumar
Illustrated by: Suman S. Roy, Tanoy Choudhury
Colouring done by: Vinay Kumar, Kiran Kumari & Pradeep Kumar

ASIA

CONTENTS

Introduction 3

Geography 5

History 8

The people 11

Climate 12

Religion 14

Festivals 16

Famous people 25

Test Your Memory 31

Index 32

Introduction

The continent of Asia is the world's largest and most populous continent. Asia also contains the world's most populous country, China and the world's largest country, Russia. Asia borders Africa and Europe in the west and is bordered by the Pacific Ocean in the east.

Asia is rich in diverse races, cultures and languages. It is also the birthplace of many major religions of the world.

Astonishing fact

The highest point on Earth, Mt. Everest is in Asia. The lowest point on land, the Dead Sea, is also in Asia!

ASIA

Asia is the only continent that borders two other continents— Africa and Europe. It sometimes joins with a third continent, North America, in winter by ice which forms in the Bering Sea. Europe and Asia are sometimes together called **Eurasia**.

The Isthmus of Suez connects Asia to Africa. The boundary between Asia and Europe runs through the Dardanelles, the Sea of Marmara, the Bosporus, to the Black Sea, the Caucasus Mountains, the Caspian Sea, the Ural River, and the Ural Mountains to the Kara Sea at Kara, Russia. It covers an estimated 44,936,000 km2 or about one-third of the world's total land area.

> Asia is almost 30 per cent of the worlds land area and contains 60 per cent of the world's population.

Geography

The Asian landmass stretches from the equator to far above the Arctic Circle. It reaches almost halfway around the globe!

Lying almost entirely in the northern hemisphere, Asia is bounded on the north by the Arctic Ocean, on the east by the Bering Strait and the Pacific Ocean, on the south by the Indian Ocean and on the southwest by the Red Sea and the Mediterranean Sea.

Its westernmost point is Cape Baba in north-western Turkey and its easternmost point is Cape Dezhnyov in north-eastern Siberia. The continent's greatest width from east to west is about 8,500 km.

> The word Asia entered English, via Latin, from Ancient Greek. This name is first mentioned in Herodotus' work (c. 440 BC), where it refers to Asia Minor.

To the southeast of the mainland is an array of archipelagos and islands extending east to the Oceanic and Australian realms. Among these islands are those of Indonesia and the Philippines, including Sumatra, Java, Celebes, Borneo and New Guinea. To the north lie Taiwan, Japan and Sakhalin. Sri Lanka and smaller island groups such as the Maldives and the Andaman and Nicobar islands are present in the Indian Ocean.

ASIA

Asia is divided into **five** major regions as follows:

- Asia of the former Soviet Union including Siberia, western Central Asia and the Caucasus Mountains
- East Asia, including China, Mongolia, Korea and Japan
- Southeast Asia, including Burma, Thailand, Cambodia, Laos, Vietnam, Malaysia, Singapore, Indonesia, Brunei, and the Philippines
- South Asia, including India, Bangladesh, Pakistan, Sri Lanka, Nepal and Bhutan
- Southwest Asia, including Afghanistan, Iran, Iraq, Turkey, Syria, Lebanon, Israel, Jordan, Saudi Arabia and the other states of the Arabian Peninsula.

Unlike the other continents, Asia has an interior that consists of mountains, plateaus and intervening structural plains fed by rivers. The highland region which is also the geographical centre of the continent is composed of the Himalaya and the associated ranges and the Tibetan Plateau. Almost all of the world's highest mountains are located in the Himalayan range. Around this region are aligned four major plateau regions (Siberia, eastern China, southern India and the Arabian Peninsula) and several great structural basins and river plains.

The Himalyas

Geography

Caspian Sea

Asia's rivers, among the longest in the world, generally rise in the high plateaus and break through the great chains toward the lowlands. They include the Ob-Irtysh, the Yenisei-Argana, and Lena of Siberia; the Amur-Argun, Huang He, Chang (Yangtze), Xi, Mekong, Thanlwin, and Ayeyarwady of East and Southeast Asia; and the Ganges-Brahmaputra, Indus, and Tigris-Euphrates of South and Southwest Asia. In Central Asia, the Amu Darya, Syr Darya, Ili and Tarim rivers empty into inland lakes or disappear into desert sands.

The world's largest lake, the **Caspian Sea**, is located in Asia. The Aral Sea, Lake Baikal and Lake Balkhash are among the world's largest lakes in Asia. Lake Baikal, in south-central Siberia, is more than 1,600 m deep—the world's deepest body of inland water.

ASIA

Indus Valley Ruins

History

Ancient civilizations

While Africa is generally regarded as the birthplace of the human species, Asia is believed to be the cradle of civilization. The coastal boundary of the continent was home to some of the world's earliest known civilizations, each of which flourished around fertile river valleys. The civilizations in Mesopotamia, the Indus Valley and the Yangtze shared many similarities and likely exchanged technologies and ideas such as mathematics and the wheel.

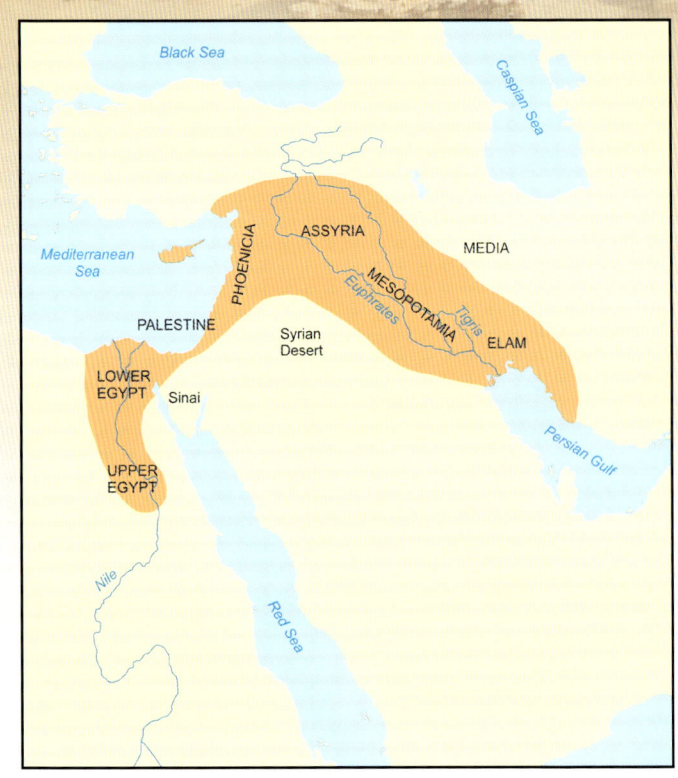

Mesopotamian civilization

The empires of Sumer, Babylonia, Assyria, Media, and Persia and the civilizations of Islam flourished in Southwest Asia, while in the east the ancient civilizations of India, China and Japan prospered. Later, nomadic tribes (Huns, Mongols and Turks) in North and Central Asia established great empires.

History

Colonialism

The Portuguese explorer Vasco da Gama reached India by sea in 1498, beginning the era of European imperialism in Asia. With the formation of English, French, Dutch and Portuguese trading companies in the 17th Century, great trade rivalry developed along the coasts of India, Southeast Asia and China resulting in an increasing European control of Asian lands.

Vasco da Gama

ASIA

By exploiting local disputes and utilizing a technological edge brought on by the industrial revolution, European powers extended political control over the Indian subcontinent and Southwest and Southeast Asia. This led to the rise of colonialism. Colonialism is the practice of forcibly establishing partial or full control over another country, nation or people. Many countries in Europe like Britain, France and Portugal etc. formed colonies in Asia.

The World War I led to the weakening of European stature in Asia. World War II and the conflicts of its aftermath hit Asia heavily too.

At the end of World War II the United States, Britain, France and the Netherlands were still major forces in Asia. But in the post-war period India, Japan, China, Indonesia and other Asian nations sought a more independent role on the world scene.

World War II

World War II

The people

The people of Asia belong to a large variety of ethnic groups. India itself is made up of several hundred groups. India's ethnic composition is so complex that the people generally identify themselves by their religion rather than their ethnic group.

A few countries, notably North Korea, South Korea and Japan are among the world's most ethnically homogeneous (made up of people belonging to the same ethnic group). The Chinese are a numerous and important ethnic group in Asia.

ASIA

Climate

The climate of the continent is varied because of its huge size. Climate in Asia range from that of the equatorial rain forest to that of the Arctic tundra.

The northern part of Asia experiences long and harsh winters, short and cool summers and light annual precipitation. A similar climate is characteristic of the Tibetan Plateau and other uplands.

The interior regions have semiarid climates, with harsh winters and warm to hot summers and an average annual rainfall of less than 230 mm.

The southern and eastern extremes of the continent are characterized by monsoonal air movements from east and south in winters and from the oceans in summer. Mostly the margins of Asia have cool to cold, dry winters and hot, humid summers, with a strong concentration of rainfall in the summer months.

Climate

In other parts of southern and eastern Asia, rainfall is either less heavily concentrated in the summer or evenly distributed throughout the year.

In places where mountains or highland obstructions interfere, the winter is likely to be wet, as is the case along the eastern coasts of portions of the Philippines, Vietnam, and Malaysia and in parts of southern India. The coastal areas of eastern Asia are also subject to destructive **typhoons**, which originate in the western Pacific and the northern part of the South China Sea.

Southwest Asia falls into a different climatic regime, experiencing winter rainfall and then passing into northern India. The average annual rainfall is light and semiarid steppe and desert climates prevail. This type of climate extends into the north-western Indian Peninsula.

Religion

Asia has been a homeland to almost all the principal religions of the world and many minor ones as well. Judaism, Christianity and Islam originated in Southwest Asia; Buddhism and Hinduism in India; and Chinese religion with Confucian and Taoist elements, as well as ancestor worship, originated in China.

Buddist monks

Christianity is today practiced by only a small number of Asians (most notably in the Philippines and South Korea). Christians form more than half the population of Cyprus and Lebanon and probably almost half that of Asiatic Russia. They are found in smaller numbers in other countries, especially in the Middle East and in former colonial areas.

Buddhism extends through interior Asia and into Southeast Asia, where it is the main religion of Burma, Thailand, Cambodia, and Laos; it also is important in Japan, Vietnam, and China. Islam is the main religion in Southwest and Central Asia and is of major importance in South Asia, where both Pakistan and Bangladesh are predominantly Muslim. Indonesia, in Southeast Asia, is also predominantly Muslim. Several Southwest Asian cities are important centres of religious pilgrimage, most prominently Mecca, Medina and Jerusalem.

Mecca

Religion

Hindus form the largest single religious group, about one-fifth of the total population. They are concentrated in the Indian subcontinent, where their religion originated. Muslims, a vast majority in southwestern and central Asia and Confucians, centered in China, are the next majority.

Jews, formerly widespread throughout the Middle East, have largely disappeared from Muslim countries since the founding of the state of Israel.

Other major Asian religions include Shintoism, in Japan; Taoism, in China; Sikhism in India and Pakistan; and Zoroastrianism, now represented mainly by the Parses in India.

A Hindu temple

Akshardham Temple

Festivals

Chinese New Year

The Chinese New Year usually takes place on the first day of the Lunar Year; in 2009 it occured on January 26. It's the most important festival in China and Taiwan and it also celebrated in Korea, Mongolia, Nepal, Bhutan and Vietnam.

During the celebrations there are lots of fireworks and people exchange gifts, decorate their houses. The occasion is marked by traditional food and clothing.

Houses are decorated with red colour paper to represent happiness, wealth and longevity. On the Eve of Chinese New Year families across the country enjoy a feast with delicacies.

The night is celebrated with firecrackers and in the morning of the New Year children receive money in red paper envelopes to symbolize a promise for the future.

New year celebrations in China

Festivals

Ati Atihan Festival

purchase by holding a massive feast and painting themselves black to look like the islanders.

Holi Festival

Holi festival is celebrated on the 5 day after the full moon in the month of March every year. This festival is primarily celebrated in India and Nepal. It is a very popular festival and is celebrated in many other parts of the world as well. Holi was originally a spring festival of fertility and harvest. To celebrate, large bonfires are also burned during the festival.

Ati Atihan Festival

The Ati-Atihan Festival is usually held in January in Philippines. It's a 2 weeks festival. The dates of Ati Atihan vary from one town to another.

The festival is celebrated because according to a legend, a group of Malay Datus (royal personages), fleeing from Borneo, bought land from the local Panay people, the original inhabitants of Panay Island. The Malay Datus celebrated their

Holi celebration

Holi is also known as the festival of colours since on this day people apply coloured powder on each other's faces and throw water balloons or squirt water with their water guns.

ASIA

Pingxi Lantern Festival

Pingxi Lantern Festival

The Pingxi Lantern Festival is a Chinese Lantern Festival which occurs every year in the month of February for six days in the town of Pingxi near Taipei, Taiwan. The festival ends on 28th February.

The main feature of this festival is the releasing of Chinese lanterns into the air creating a magical sea of lights. The history of Chinese lanterns began during the Ching Dynasty when bands of outlaws frequently raided Taiwans villages around Pingxi. Local residents would seek refuge in the mountains. The Sky Lanterns were signals used by the village watchmen to inform the residents that the village was once again safe.

Cherry Blossom Festival

The Cherry Blossom Festival is a festival which takes place from January to May across the different areas of Japan depending on when the cherry blossoms open up.

This time of the year is the best time to visit Japan as the country looks like a land form from a fairytale. The Japanese people picnic among the Cherry trees throughout the day and also by the moonlight.

Cherry Blossom Festival

Festivals

Naadam Festival

The Naadam is celebrated all over Mongolia in the Midsummer holiday of July 11-13th. The dates can sometimes vary. Nadaam and its traditional games are believed to be almost two thousand years old but the festival as it exists today is celebrated to commemorate the 1921 revolution when Mongolia declared itself a free country.

Naadam Festival

During the festival one can witness Mongolian wrestling in which the wrestling has no time limit and the most famous wrestler chooses his own opponent. Other events that take place are horse racing and archery.

ASIA

Decoration of hands with mehendi

Eid Al-Fitr

Eid Al Fitr is an Islamic festival (often referred to as Eid). The festival celebrates the end of Ramadan the holy month of mourning and fasting. The date of Eid is determined by the appearance of crescent shaped moon in the sky.

During the festival there is a great sense of community feeling as people eat and pray together. Gifts are exchanged between family, friends and colleagues and people dress up in their best clothes. People visit the graves of their ancestors and deceased member to offer homage to them.

Eid is the Arabic word for festivity and Fitr means to breakfast. So the festival marks the feast of breakfast.

Eid celebrations

Festivals

Monkey Festival

Monkey Festival of Thailand

The Monkey Festival is celebrated on the last Sunday of the month of November in the Pra Prang Sam Yot temple in Lopburi, Thailand.

Lot of Macaque monkeys come down to the Pra Prang Buddhist Temple to enjoy the feast offered by the people of the town.

The festival is a tribute to the Monkey God Hanuman who was awarded the province by Lord Rama.

ASIA

Diwali

Diwali or Deepavali, also known as the 'festival of lights' is a Hindu festival that usually takes place in Mid-October/November and is celebrated by the Hindus worldwide. The festival is celebrated on the night of New Moon. Traditionally the festival lasts for five days. The most famous event of the festival includes a night time display of candles, lamps and fireworks.

The word Diwali comes from the Sanskrit word Deepavali which means a 'rows of lights.'

The festival celebrates the victory of good over evil, light over darkness and knowledge over ignorance.

Earthen lamps are lit to help the Goddess Lakshmi find her way into people's homes. They also celebrate one of the Diwali legends, which tell of the return of Lord Rama and his wife Sita to their kingdom after fourteen years of exile.

Fireworks are a big part of the Diwali celebrations, although in recent years there has been a move against them because of noise, atmospheric pollution and the number of accidental deaths and injuries.

The legend of Diwali

Ravana, who had ten arms and ten heads, was the wicked king of the island of Sri Lanka, who had kidnapped Sita, the wife of Lord Rama. Rama had been in exile for 14 years because of a disagreement as to whether he or his brother should be the next king in Ayodhya.

After a great battle Rama killed the demon and recovered his wife. Rama's return with his wife Sita to Ayodhya and his subsequent coronation as the king, is celebrated at Diwali.

Rakhi

Raksha Bandhan

Raksha Bandhan is a Hindu festival which celebrates the love between a brother and his sister. The word **Raksha** means 'protection' and **Bandhan** means to 'tie'. During the festival sisters tie a **rakhi**, a holy bracelet made of interwoven threads, around their brothers' wrists to celebrate their relationship.

It is believed that when a woman ties a rakhi around the hand of a man it becomes his religious duty to protect her.

Sisters tie the sacred Rakhi string on their brothers' right wrists and pray for their long life.

Famous people

Attila the Hun

Attila the Hun was the leader of the Hunnish Empire, which stretched from Germany to the Ural River and from the Danube River to the Baltic Sea from A.D. 433 to 453. During his rule, he was one of the most fearsome enemies of the Western and Eastern Roman Empire. He was known as the 'Scourge of God' by the Romans. Succeeding his uncle, King Roas, in 433, Attila shared his throne with his brother Bleda. Attila's first task was to unite his subjects for the purpose of creating one of the most formidable and feared armies Asia had ever seen.

He is popularly known for his two aggressive military campaigns in the last two years of his life which threatened to dramatically redirect the development of Western Europe.

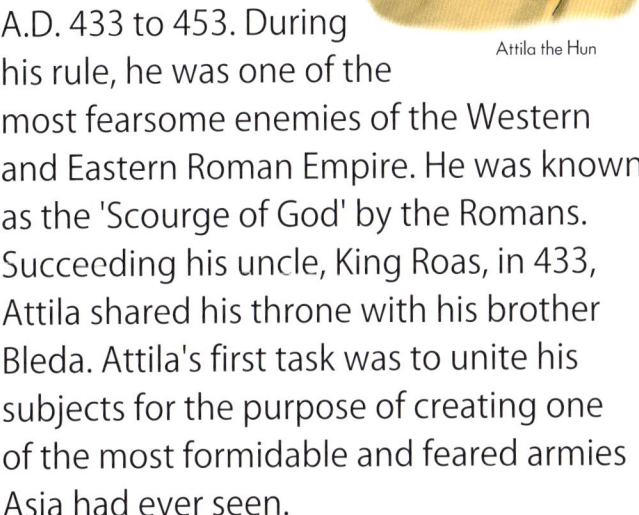
Attila the Hun

Confucius

Confucius was a thinker, political figure, educator and founder of the Ru School of Chinese thought. He was born in 551 BC, and his parents were poor, although his family had once been rich. Confucius is a modification of the name K'ung Fu-tzu. Although, K'ung Fu-tzu was the philosopher's correct name, he has historically been referred to as Confucius in Western countries.

The religion of Confucianism derives its name from Confucius and is based on his writings. These writings were intended to be advice for the rulers of China in the sixth century BCE, and were later studied by the followers of Confucius. In addition, his followers brought in ideas originating in Buddhism and Taoism, as Confucianism spread from China to other Asian countries, including Korea, Japan and Vietnam.

One idea emphasized by Confucius was 'beautiful conduct'. He thought that if everyone in a society could achieve 'beautiful conduct', or what he considered correct behaviour, society could become perfect. This involved avoiding all extreme actions and emotions, being considerate to others, respecting family and worshiping ancestors.

Confucius

Asoka the Great

Eight years after he took his throne, Asoka's powerful armies attacked and conquered Kalinga (present day Orissa). Although Asoka had conquered many other places, this violent war was the last war he ever fought and this was a turning point of his career. He was disgusted by the deaths of numerous civilians, especially the Brahmans. All these misfortunes changed Asoka into a religious ruler.

As he turned to Buddhism, he emphasized dharma (law of piety) and ahimsa (nonviolence). He realized he could not spread Buddhism all by himself and therefore appointed officers to help promote the teachings.

Asoka the Great

Asoka was one of the most powerful kings of the Indian subcontinent. He ruled over the country from 273 BC to 232 BC. The reign of Emperor Asoka covered most of India, South Asia and beyond, stretching from present day Afghanistan and parts of Persia in the west, to Bengal and Assam in the east and Mysore in the south.

As the third emperor of the Mauryan dynasty, his greatest achievements were spreading Buddhism throughout his empire and beyond. He set up an ideal government for his people and conquered many lands, expanding his kingdom.

Asoka's edict

Mao Zedong

Mao Zedong is considered to be the father of Communist China and alongside Sun Yat-sen and Chiang Kai-shek who played a fundamental part in China's recent history. Mao Zedong was the son of a peasant farmer born in Chaochan, China, in 1893. He became a Marxist while working as a library assistant at the Peking University and served in the revolutionary army during the 1911 Chinese Revolution.

The China that Mao ZeDong was born into seemed to be falling apart. The Qin dynasty that ruled China was on the verge of collapse, and there was social and economic unrest. All this opened the doors for Mao to become its leader one day.

Mao's greatest achievements were the unification of China, the creation of a unified Republic of China and becoming the leader of the greatest social revolution in history. The revolution involved taking over most of the land and property, destroying the landlord class, weakening the middle class and raising the status of the peasant and industrial workers.

Mao believed in the ability of the peasants and workers to organize and rule, which was the core reason for the success of communism in China.

Gandhi

Mohandas Karamchand Gandhi is considered the father of the Indian independence movement against British rule. His doctrine of non-violent protest to achieve political and social progress has been hugely influential.

Gandhi spent twenty years in South Africa working to fight discrimination. It was there that he created his concept of **satyagraha**, a non-violent way of protesting against injustices.

While in India, Gandhi's obvious virtue, simplistic lifestyle and minimal dress made him closer to the people. He spent his remaining years working diligently to both remove British rule from India as well as to better the lives of India's poorest classes. Many civil rights leaders, including Martin Luther King Jr. and Nelson Mandela used Gandhi's concept of non-violent protest as a model for their struggles.

Gandhi is still a worldwide considered to be an icon of non-violent political resistance. He was given the title of **Mahatma**, the Hindu term for 'great soul' by the nobel laureate Rabindranath Tagore.

Famous people

Dalai Lama

His Holiness the Dalai Lama is the highest-ranking lama (spiritual master) of Tibetan Buddhism. The current Dalai Lama is the fourteenth of his line, and was born to a farming family in 1935 and given the name Lhamo Dhondrub. He was recognized at the age of two, and brought with his family to live in Lhasa, the capital of Tibet at the age of four, where he became His Holiness the 14th Dalai Lama Tenzin Gyatso. (Dalai Lamas, like Popes, change names upon taking up their office.) He was reared and educated in the monastery system.

When China annexed Tibet in 1959, the Dalai Lama and thousands of his supporters fled into exile. He has been living in Dharamsala, India, since 1960 and heads the Tibetan government-in-exile. China does not recognize Tibet as an independent political entity.

The Dalai Lama has been a powerful spokesman for Tibet, and Buddhism in general, and has written a number of books on the topic. His consistent opposition to violence was recognized in 1989 with the Nobel Peace Prize.

Lhasa, Tibet

Aung San Suu Kyi

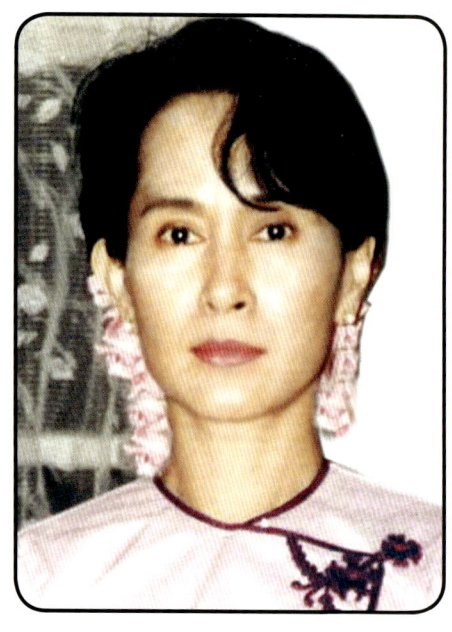

Aung San Suu Kyi (Awn-Sahn-Sue-Chee) is Burma's pro-democracy leader and opposition politician. She has been fighting against the rule of the junta, a group of military leaders who have been ruling over Burma (now Myanmar) almost ever since the country got its independence from the British. She was arrested for her campaign against the millitary government and has spent more than 15 years in detention, most of it under house arrest. She was released from her current third period of detention on Saturday November 13, 2010.

Aung San Suu Kyi was born on June 19th, 1945 as the daughter of Burma's independence hero, Aung San, who was assassinated when she was only two years old. She received the Nobel Peace Prize in 1991 for her political efforts. In 1992 she was awarded the Jawaharlal Nehru Award for International Understanding by the government of India and the International Simón Bolívar Prize from the government of Venezuela. Aung San Suu Kyi has come to symbolise the struggle of Burma's people to be free.

Test Your MEMORY

1. What are the highest point and the lowest point on Earth?
2. Asia is the only continent that borders two other continents. What are the names of those continents?
3. Which piece of land connects Asia to Africa?
4. In which year did the Portuguese explorer Vasco da Gama reached India?
5. Which country in Asia is the birthplace of Buddhism and Hinduism?
6. In which country is the Ati-Atihan festival celebrated?
7. In which month of the year is the Holi festival celebrated?
8. In which country the Pingxi Lantern Festival celebrated?
9. Which festival has been nicknamed 'the festival of lights'?
10. What does the name Buddha mean?
11. Who was Confucius?
12. In which year was the current Dalai Lama awarded the Nobel Prize?

Index

A
Africa 3, 4, 8, 28
Ati-Atihan 17

B
borders 3, 4

C
China 3, 6, 8, 9, 10, 13, 14, 15, 16, 25, 27, 29
civilization 8
climate 12, 13
colonialism 9, 10
Confucius 25

D
Dalai Lama 29

E
East Asia 3, 6
Eid 20
empires 8
equator 5
Eurasia 4
Europe 3, 4, 10, 25
explorer 9

F
festival 17, 18, 19, 21, 31

G
Gandhi 28

H
hemisphere 5
Himalaya 6
Holi 17

I
imperialism 9
industrial revolution 10
Isthmus of Suez 4

L
Lantern Festival 18

M
Mao Zedong 27
Mediterranean Sea 5

P
Pacific 3, 5, 13

R
rakhi 24
Ramadan 20
religions 3, 14, 15
Russia 3, 4, 14

S
Southeast Asia 6, 7, 10, 14
Southwest Asia 6, 7, 8, 13, 14

T
typhoons 13

W
World War 10

---

* Maps not to scale; for illustration purpose only.